W9-BRA-619

PROPERTY OF SCHOOL
DISTRICT NO. 75

women's track and field

Consultant

Will Stephens, coach
Will's Spiketts Track Team
Carmichael, California

Demonstrators

Members of Will's Spiketts
Track Team

published by:
The Athletic Institute
Merchandise Mart, Chicago

*A not-for-profit organization
devoted to the advancement of
athletics, physical education
and recreation.*

Robert G. Bluth, editor

© The Athletic Institute 1973
All Rights Reserved

**Library of Congress
Catalog Card Number 79-109498**

**"Sports Techniques" Series
SBN 87670-077-6**

**Published by The Athletic Institute
Chicago, Illinois 60654**

Foreword

The SPORTS TECHNIQUES SERIES is but one item in a comprehensive list of sports instructional aids which are made available by The Athletic Institute. This book is part of a master plan which seeks to make the benefits of athletics, physical education and recreation available to everyone.

The Athletic Institute is a not-for-profit organization devoted to the advancement of athletics, physical education and recreation. The Institute believes that participation in athletics and recreation has benefits of inestimable value to the individual and to the community.

The nature and scope of the many Institute programs are determined by a *Professional Advisory Committee,* whose members are noted for their outstanding knowledge, experience and ability in the fields of athletics, physical education and recreation.

The Institute believes that through this book the reader will become a better performer, skilled in the fundamentals of this fine event. Knowledge and the practice necessary to mold knowledge into playing ability are the keys to real enjoyment in playing any game or sport.

Women's track and field events aid in the development of motor skill, flexibility, agility and endurance as well as providing enjoyable recreation.

Donald E. Bushore
Executive Director
The Athletic Institute

Introduction

Most all track and field events provide women with a challenging opportunity to develop and experience the extremes of physical and mental effort. The diverse elements of this sport call for power, accuracy, stamina, agility, finesse, concentration and determination. The challenge, fascination and satisfaction derived through participation have allowed women possessing varied levels of skill to enjoy these activities in our country and throughout the world.

Primarily, this book is written for the beginning coach or athlete in the belief that if the individual learns to perform her event correctly during the primary stages of her track and field participation, opportunity for success and advanced development is greatly increased.

As the athlete progresses, this book then serves as a good review of those fundamentals and techniques essential to success.

Will Stephens

Table of Contents

Table of Contents (continued)

starts

The Starting Blocks

Standard starting blocks afford the sprinter the possibility of a strong, fast start.

Blocks vary as to styling and material, but most generally are of one-piece construction and are adjustable to personal desires and specifications of the performer.

1. STANDARD STARTING BLOCKS USUALLY ARE OF ONE-PIECE CONSTRUCTION AND ARE ADJUSTABLE TO PERSONAL REQUIREMENTS.
2. BECOME FAMILIAR WITH THE COMMON TYPES OF BLOCKS WHICH YOU MAY BE CALLED UPON TO USE.
3. RIGHT-HANDED SPRINTERS SHOULD HAVE RIGHT "POWER" LEG BACK AND LEFT LEG ABOUT 8 TO 12 INCHES IN FRONT.

Sprint Start Techniques

Make the necessary starting block adjustments suited to your starting style and comfort.

First call is "Runners, Stand at Your Marks," or a command of a similar nature.

"Runners Go to Your Marks"

Upon this command from the starter, stand in front or straddle the blocks with feet even with the back-facing of the blocks.

To help relax your leg muscles, you may choose to stretch your muscles by extending each leg backward before placing your feet in the blocks. The back foot is inserted first, then the front foot. Be certain that the tips of the toes contact the ground.

Lower the knee of the back leg beside the foot of the forward leg. Lean forward to place your hands behind the starting line, a shoulder's-width apart.

Adjust feet and hands for comfort. Note that the arms are straight and even with the forward knee. Fingers and thumb form a "V."

Take a deep breath then let it out slowly to relax. Body weight should be back toward the rear foot.

1. **STRADDLE BLOCKS WITH EACH FOOT EVEN WITH THE BACK FACING OF BLOCK.**

2. **STRETCH LEGS BACKWARD TO RELAX MUSCLES BEFORE PLACING FEET IN BLOCKS. INSERT BACK FOOT FIRST, THEN FORWARD FOOT.**

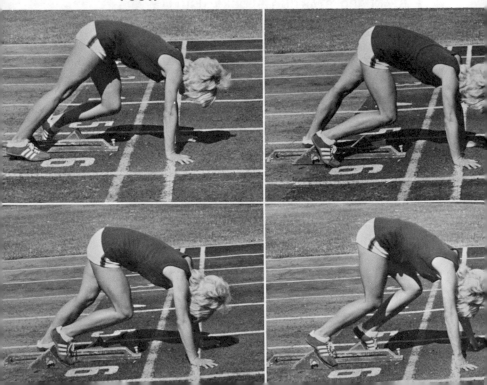

3. **LOWER KNEE OF BACK LEG BESIDE FOOT OF FORWARD LEG. LEAN FORWARD TO PLACE HANDS BEHIND STARTING LINE AT A SHOULDER'S-WIDTH APART.**

4. **ADJUST FEET AND HANDS FOR COMFORT. FINGERS AND THUMB FORM "V" FACING FINISHING LINE.**

5. **TAKE DEEP BREATH, THEN LET IT OUT TO RELAX. WEIGHT IS SLIGHTLY TOWARD BACK LEG AND FOOT. FOCUS EYES DOWNWARD OR A FEW FEET IN FRONT.**

"Set"

After this command raise your hips approximately shoulder high to shift weight over your hands.

The foreleg portion of the back leg should be about parallel with the ground. The forward knee forms a 90-degree angle.

Focus your eyes some eight to 10 yards down the track. Take a deep breath and block out actions of competitors and extraneous noises. Concentrate only on getting a good start.

6. **RAISE HIPS TO SHOULDER HEIGHT, SHIFTING WEIGHT OVER HANDS.**

7. FORELEG OF BACK LEG NEARLY PARALLEL WITH GROUND. FORWARD KNEE FORMS 90-DEGREE ANGLE.
8. FOCUS EYES 8 TO 10 YARDS DOWN TRACK. TAKE DEEP BREATH. CONCENTRATE ONLY ON GOOD START.

The Gun ("Go")

React instantly to the firing of the gun by exhaling forcefully, driving from the blocks with both legs and projecting the front leg to a full extension.

The back knee drives forward and slightly upward as the opposite arm shoots forward and then back out in front, slightly above the eyes in a "vicious" action. The opposite arm is also "cocked" at a 90-degree angle and follows with natural action. The forward leg exerts great pressure against the front block to extend fully off the block.

First stride from the blocks should be as long as can be effectively controlled. Eyes are focused about three to five yards in front.

Keep the angle of your body low to the ground. The first strides are shorter but not choppy. The natural forward lean of the body will cause the stride to be shorter until the normal, upright position is achieved.

Drive arms vigorously for balance and keep knees high. Learn to relax. By relaxing you run with longer strides resulting in better times.

9. DRIVE FORWARD LEG OFF BLOCK TO FULL EXTENSION, DRIVE FORWARD NOT UP. AT GUN, EXPLODE FROM BLOCKS BY EXHALING FORCEFULLY.
10. PROJECT REAR LEG AND OPPOSITE ARM FORWARD THEN BACK IN A VICIOUS ACTION.
11. BODY ANGLE LOW TO GROUND FOR FIRST 10 TO 15 YARDS. AS ONE ARM PROJECTS FORWARD TOWARD THE FINISH LINE AND PARALLEL WITH GROUND, THE OPPOSITE ARM AND HAND SWING BACK TO HEIGHT EVEN WITH HIP.
12. DRIVE ARMS VIGOROUSLY TO AID BALANCE.
13. RUN RELAXED. ELONGATE STRIDE ONCE NATURAL, UPRIGHT RUNNING POSITION IS ACHIEVED.

The Bunch Start

Some sprinters prefer to start from blocks spaced more closely together.

For the *Bunch Start,* the blocks are spaced about six to eight inches apart.

Regardless of how far you prefer to space the blocks, your success in starting depends greatly on reaction time, strength and application of basic techniques.

Practice often to fully develop your starting capability.

1. SPACE BLOCKS ABOUT 6 TO 8 INCHES APART FOR BUNCH START.
2. APPLY ALL SPRINT START TECHNIQUES AS PREVIOUSLY DESCRIBED.

Start for Middle Distance and Long Distance Runs

Sprints are those races up to and including the 440-yard dash. Some coaches prefer to think of the 440 as a middle distance race, especially at the high school level since many runners lack the physical capability to run the race completely as a sprint. Nevertheless, the sprint start is used for the 440 as it is for races of less distance.

The 880-yard run is truly a middle distance race in which the runner may wish to use a modified sprint start or a standing start.

A runner choosing to use blocks for the 880 or even the 440 is not required to explode out of the blocks to the extent that the sprinter must. By using blocks, the runner wants to make sure that her start is smooth and clean.

The standing start is used for distance of a mile and longer. For races of those distances, the standing start is preferred because it requires considerably less energy. Furthermore, the start is of lesser importance for longer races than for a sprint.

How a runner starts from a standing position is almost wholly a matter of personal preference. Some runners prefer to lean slightly forward at the waist with one foot in back of the other, while others feel comfortable and get better results by crouching more forward.

This is not to say that the start for a long distance run isn't important. Quite the contrary, a good start often means a good position relative to the rest of the field which eventually may prove to be an important factor in winning.

sprinting and distance running

Because of individual differences in physical makeup, the form of one runner is slightly different from that of another. Therefore, running form can be described only in general terms.

Body Angle When Running

Once a steady running speed is attained, the body angle tends toward the perpendicular. A slight forward lean may be necessary when running into a wind—the stronger the wind, the greater the lean. Most runners, from sprints to the mile run, use a very erect body carriage once a steady speed is achieved. When the rate of acceleration in sprinting is greatest, the forward lean also must be at its greatest. The sprinter has a tremendous forward lean at the start of her run. From the instant the sprinter starts to the point of top speed, the rate of acceleration gradually diminishes as speed increases. The degree of forward lean becomes less as top speed is approached. At top speed, in the absence of wind resistance, there would be no lean at all. However, a runner travelling some 20 miles per hour at top speed on a perfectly calm and windless day creates her own wind resistance. She requires a slight forward lean to offset the resistance but not much.

1. FORWARD LEAN GREATEST WHEN ACCELERATING.
2. ONCE RUNNING SPEED IS ACHIEVED, BODY ANGLE TENDS TOWARD THE PERPENDICULAR.
3. SLIGHT FORWARD LEAN MAY BE NECESSARY WHEN RUNNING INTO WIND.

Head Position

The head is directed to the front, bent neither forward nor backward and held in natural alignment with the body. If individual considerations cause you to run with your head high because it is uncomfortable any other way, you should be permitted to do so providing it does not cause you to lean backward or otherwise decrease your rate of forward progress.

1. **RUN WITH HEAD DIRECTED TO THE FRONT, BENT NEITHER FORWARD NOR BACKWARD.**

2. **INDIVIDUAL PREFERENCE MAY PERMIT SLIGHT CHANGE IN HEAD POSITION PROVIDING FORWARD PROGRESS IS NOT AFFECTED.**

Arm Action

Arm action plays a balancing role in running. As the right leg strides forward, the right shoulder moves back and the left shoulder, forward. The left arm comes forward, around the body, while the right arm moves back. As the left leg comes forward, the movement of the arms is reversed.

Arm action must be around the body in a forward direction and must not hinder the running progression. The lower arm comes forward with each step. Higher arm action is faster than lower arm action. Higher arm action is usually associated with faster leg action although the legs actually lead the arms.

However, at the finish of the race when the legs are weak from fatigue, the arms are used to drive the legs faster. Action and reaction of the legs and arms are interchangeable.

The arm action must be a natural movement, devoid of unnatural tension. If the arms get tired quickly or ache while running, perhaps they are being held in an unnatural position or are subjected to unnecessary tension.

The hands are held in a relaxed "cup" position, not in a tight fist.

1. **AS THE RIGHT LEG STRIDES FORWARD, LEFT ARM COMES FORWARD AND AROUND BODY WHILE RIGHT ARM MOVES BACK.**

2. **SEQUENCE IS REVERSED WHEN LEFT LEG STRIDES FORWARD. UPPER ARM ACTION FASTER THAN LOWER ARM ACTION.**

3. **ARM ACTION IS A NATURAL MOVEMENT, DEVOID OF TENSION.**

4. **HANDS HELD IN RELAXED, "CUP" POSITION.**

Leg Action

Leg action propels the body forward.

The forward foot contacts the track directly under the body's projected center of gravity. The knee of the forward leg is bent at the moment of contact. The outer edge of the ball of the foot makes first contact with the track. Immediately thereafter the heel touches the track. Any muscular effort to prevent the heel from touching the track is positively unnatural and should be discouraged.

Power should be applied over the greatest possible foot area to achieve maximum acceleration—thus if the heel does not touch the track for at least an "instant" when running at any distance, then power cannot be applied over the greatest possible area to achieve maximum acceleration.

During the instant that the foot is flat upon the track, it bears the runner's full weight, and the body rides smoothly forward for the next stride. Actually, the foot has come to a complete stop for an instant. As the body weight continues to ride forward over the bent knee, the heel first is lifted and then as the knee is fully extended (straightened) the toe leaves the track for the next stride. Briefly, the action of the foot is ball, heel, ball in landing and leaving the track.

1. **OUTER EDGE OF BALL OF FOOT MAKES FIRST CONTACT FOLLOWED INSTANTLY BY HEEL. ATTEMPTING TO PREVENT HEEL FROM CONTACTING TRACK IF ONLY SLIGHTLY IS UNNATURAL.**
2. **FORWARD FOOT CONTACTS TRACK DIRECTLY UNDER PROJECTED CENTER OF GRAVITY.**
3. **HEEL CONTACT HELPS TO PROVIDE MAXIMUM LEVERAGE FOR ACCELERATION AND HELPS TO RELAX LEG MUSCLES.**
4. **KNEE IS BENT UPON CONTACT.**
5. **SEQUENCE OF FOOT ACTION IS "BALL, HEEL, BALL."**

Stride Length

Quite often, stride length is misunderstood. The slower the speed of the run, the shorter the stride length should be. The faster the run, the longer the stride.

A runner takes the longest stride when sprinting and decreases the stride length when running more slowly. Sprinters take the longest strides and marathon runners, the shortest.

Longer strides are faster but require far more energy. A sprinter is not concerned primarily with conservation of energy, therefore uses the longer, faster but less-economical long stride.

As the racing distance increases, economy of effort becomes more important. Athletes naturally adjust the stride length accordingly. Two short strides carry the runner farther than one long stride and they require far less energy.

In races longer than the sprints, wherein economy of stride motion is a prime consideration, a runner should take a natural step—not exaggerated, not short, but a natural step in keeping with maximum economy of effort for the speed required.

1. **THE SLOWER THE SPEED OF RUN, THE SHORTER THE STRIDE.**
2. **CONVERSELY, THE FASTER THE RUN, THE LONGER THE STRIDE.**

3. LONGER STRIDES REQUIRE MORE ENERGY. IN DISTANCE RACES WHERE ECONOMY OF ENERGY IS IMPORTANT, SHORTER STRIDES SHOULD BE TAKEN. HOWEVER, TAKE A NATURAL STEP NOT AN EXAGGERATED SHORT STEP.

hurdles

The Start

A sprint start is used to start a hurdle race. However, a hurdler achieves an upright running position sooner than when running a sprint.

Some hurdlers run an odd number of steps to the first hurdle while others choose to take an even number of strides. The odd or even number of steps depends on personal preference and ability.

Do not look at the first hurdle until about the fifth step. Until this time, focus your complete attention upon getting a good start.

Practice the hurdle start often.

1. ALL SPRINT START TECHNIQUES APPLY, BUT THE HURDLER ACHIEVES AN UPRIGHT RUNNING POSITION SOONER.

2. CONCENTRATE FULLY ON GETTING GOOD START. DO NOT LOOK AT FIRST HURDLE UNTIL APPROXIMATELY FIFTH STEP FROM START.

Hurdling Techniques

Lifting the lead knee straight up is most fundamental to hurdling success. This is not to say that the leg is held straight when going over the hurdle, only that the vertical lift of the knee should be in a straight line to the direction of the run.

Actually, the lead foot is kicked directly at the hurdle. Do not swing the lead leg. Throwing the front leg out to the side causes loss of distance and balance.

Most right-handed hurdlers prefer to lead with the left leg. If this is uncomfortable, try leading with the right leg. Leading with the left leg has an advantage when running hurdles on the curve.

Generally, the takeoff point is 6½ to seven feet from the hurdle. The knee of the lead leg is driven toward the hurdle and is flexed slightly.

Keep the shoulders square to the face of the hurdle.

Thrust the arm opposite the lead leg forward and slightly downward. Keep the elbows from flailing outward by turning the thumb outward as the arm starts back.

Snap the lead leg down to land on the ball of the foot. Drive off the foot for a strong first step after clearing the hurdle. Landing distance from the hurdle is about 3½ to four feet. Be sure to land on the ball of the foot, not the heel.

While going over the hurdle, the back leg lays flat with toes pointed to the side, not downward. Pull the trailing leg across the hurdle as quickly as possible. As the knee comes thru, drive the knee toward the head and "pop" the toes forward to land on ball of foot. A strong, initial kick with the lead leg helps to bring the back leg through faster.

Above all, do not swing the trailing leg around as it is brought over the hurdle.

3. **SPRINT TO TAKEOFF POINT KEEPING SHOULDERS SQUARE TO FACE OF HURDLE.**

4. **KICK LEAD FOOT AT HURDLE. LEAN FORWARD AND THRUST OPPOSITE ARM FORWARD AND SLIGHTLY DOWNWARD.**

5. **BODY BENDS OVER LEAD LEG WITH A DRIVING MOTION.**

6. **GOING OVER HURDLE, TRAILING LEG LAYS FLAT WITH TOES POINTED OUTWARD OR SLIGHTLY UPWARD.**

7. **PULL TRAILING LEG ACROSS HURDLE QUICKLY THEN DRIVE KNEE TOWARD THE HEAD AND "POP" THE TOES FORWARD TO LAND ON BALL OF FOOT.**

8. **FIRST STRIDE AFTER HURDLE SHOULD BE POWERFUL AND JUST SLIGHTLY LONGER THAN NORMAL SO THAT LAST STRIDE IS SLIGHTLY SHORTER FOR MORE POWERFUL DRIVE OVER HURDLE.**

Running Between Hurdles

As the trailing leg comes through, snap the lead leg forward and down for a good, full stride.

The first two steps should be slightly longer than the third step which precedes the next high hurdle.

A somewhat shorter third step will help keep the body in good position to lean into the hurdle during takeoff and give more power over the hurdle.

1. RUN WITH KNEES HIGH AND TAKE A SLIGHTLY LONGER STRIDE COMING OFF EACH HURDLE.

2. FIRST TWO STEPS AFTER HIGH HURDLE SOMEWHAT LONGER THAN THIRD STEP PRECEDING NEXT HURDLE. SHORTER THIRD STEP HELPS KEEP BODY IN POSITION TO LEAN INTO HURDLE DURING POWER TAKEOFF.

team relay

Apart from starting, running and finishing a team relay race, one more variable is involved—that of exchanging the baton.

The baton exchange within the passing zone with runners "flying" at top speed is one of the most exciting maneuvers in all of sport.

Starting a Sprint Relay

Hold the baton with the middle, ring and little fingers near the end. The thumb and index fingers are extended to form a "V" so as to make contact with the ground behind the starting line. The second and third knuckles rest on the ground behind.

At the sound of the gun, enclose the extended thumb and index fingers around the baton as the arms start their forward thrust.

From this point, all sprint start techniques apply.

1. **HOLD BATON WITH THREE FINGERS. INDEX FINGER AND THUMB FORM "V" TO CONTACT GROUND BEHIND STARTING LINE. SECOND AND THIRD KNUCKLES REST ON GROUND BEHIND.**

2. **AT GUN, CLOSE INDEX FINGER AND THUMB AROUND BATON AS ARMS START THRUST.**

3. APPLY ALL SPRINT START TECHNIQUES.

Receiver's Position for Receiving Baton

Some relay sprinters may prefer to start from a three-point stance, whereas others may choose to begin from a more upright stance. For purposes of this discussion, the three-point stance is preferred.

Three-Point Stance Takeoff Position

To assume the three-point stance, space your feet as though they were in starting blocks and in line to the direction of the run.

The back leg is straight with the hips held high. The left arm should be well back allowing you to see the incoming runner. From this extended position backward, the left arm is then used as a driving force to explode out of the three-point stance upon the verbal "go" command from the incoming runner.

or

1. ASSUME THREE-POINT STANCE WITH FEET SPACED AS IF IN BLOCKS AND LINED UP IN DIRECTION OF RUN.
2. BACK LEG IS STRAIGHT AND LEFT ARM EXTENDED BACK, ALLOWING YOU TO SEE INCOMING SPRINTER.

3. USE LEFT ARM TO HELP YOU EXPLODE OUT OF STANCE UPON COMMAND FROM INCOMING SPRINTER.

Receiving Arm and Hand Positions

Run forward without looking back. The receiving arm and hand are extended in line with the rear leg.

Cock the wrist forward with the fingers together and the thumb spread to form a "V" between the index finger and thumb.

Remember, don't look back during exchange. Eyes remain forward to direction of run.

1. **RUN FORWARD AND DON'T LOOK BACK. RECEIVING ARM AND HAND EXTENDED BACK IN LINE WITH REAR LEG.**

2. **COCK WRIST FORWARD WITH FINGERS TOGETHER AND FOREFINGER AND THUMB FORMING "V".**

Passing and Receiving the Baton

The sprinter passing the baton brings her baton hand in an upward motion to the receiver's hand.

The passer's baton hand is stemmed upward and into the receiver's hand while the receiver's hand is cocked in a forward position. The passer must keep her eyes on the exchange throughout the pass. Again, the receiver must continue to look forward throughout the exchange.

With the passer's hand stemmed upward, the receiver gains control of the baton with her thumb and index finger. The receiver then quickly pulls the baton through the passer's hand. The receiver secures the baton with a "milking-type" action of her fingers.

This exchange method allows the passer and receiver good control of the baton at all times. While other types of exchanges may have certain advantages, this method provides optimum security and control.

1. **PASSER BRINGS BATON UP AND STEMMED TO RECEIVER'S HAND.**
   PASSER KEEPS EYES ON EXCHANGE.

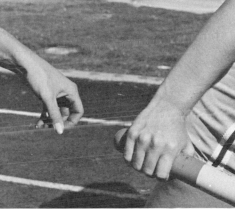

2. **RECEIVER GAINS CONTROL OF BATON WITH FOREFINGER AND THUMB TO PULL BATON QUICKLY FROM PASSER'S HAND. "MILKING-ACTION" OF FINGERS FURTHER SECURES BATON.**

3. **EXCHANGE METHOD PROVIDES SECURITY AND CONTROL.**

Exchange Tactics

Receiver (2nd Runner and 4th Runner Only)

The receiver should be in position when the incoming runner is about 40 yards from her "go" marker. At the precise moment the incoming runner reaches the marker, the receiver explodes out of her three-point stance with a terrific inside (left) arm action just as if she were accelerating out of the blocks. The receiver runs a straight line from the outside of her lane and finishes to the inside of her lane when she arrives at the first line of the exchange zone. She continues on the inside of her lane thru the exchange zone. When the receiver arrives at the first line of the exchange zone, she extends her right arm back in the receiving position. The exchange should be made within six yards after entering the exchange zone. Continue to the finish on the inside of the lane.

Passing Runner (Incoming—1st Runner and 3rd Runner Only)

The **incoming runner** runs as close to the inside line as possible until she comes to the International mark 11 yards from the exchange zone's first line.

The **passer** starts a straight-line run to the outside of the lane. She should be at the outside of her lane by the time she arrives at the first line of the exchange zone. **The receiver** at this point starts her receiving hand back while **the passer** prepares to make the exchange. **The passer** should continue on the outside of her lane, slowing down and waiting for all runners to clear.

Receiver (3rd Runner)

So as to give the **second runner** a longer run on the straightaway, the **third runner** should put the marker for the **incoming runner** at the International mark. This will cause the baton exchange to be made near the end of the zone.

The receiver should set in a three-point stance on the outside of her lane. When the **incoming runner** hits the takeoff mark, **the receiver** continues in a straight line on the outside of her lane until the exchange is made; she then cuts into the curve of her lane in a straight line after leaving the exchange zone. The **third runner** should put her left hand back halfway (middle) through the exchange zone to receive the baton.

Passing Runner (Incoming 2nd Runner)

With the baton in hand, the **second runner** should "hug" the inside of the lane coming out of the turn with the baton and stay on the inside of her lane all the way into and out of the exchange zone. The runner prepares to start the exchange midway into the exchange zone.

Working as a Team

As with the case of all team sports, team success depends on proper execution by all team members.

A relay team may have the fastest runners in the world, yet may lose to a team with slower runners because that team executes the proper strategy and tactics sufficient to win the race.

The Leadoff Sprinter

A **leadoff sprinter** should be a dependable, quick starter, and an excellent curve runner for a distance of about 105 yards.

The first runner starts with the baton in her left hand to pass to the second runner within six yards after entering the exchange zone.

The Second Sprinter

This sprinter should be the team's best straightaway runner and very strong for 121 yards.

The **second runner** receives the baton in her right hand and should plan to take the baton as soon as possible after entering the exchange zone having started from the International mark (some 11 yds. from passing zone.)

I FAN GO			
┃ ----➔ ┃	⊏⊐━━━━━━━━━━━━━━━━➔		
MARK MARK			
	11	PASSING ZONE	
	←YARDS➔	←━━━ 22 YARDS ━━━➔	

The Third Sprinter

The **third runner** should be the best receiver and passer on the team as well as a good curve runner.

She should start her run about halfway between the International mark and the beginning of the exchange zone to receive the baton in her left hand near the end of the zone.

After receiving the baton, the third runner should continue another five yards on the right side of her lane then head for the inside with a run of about 16 yards to build speed and prepare for a sprint of approximately 100 yards.

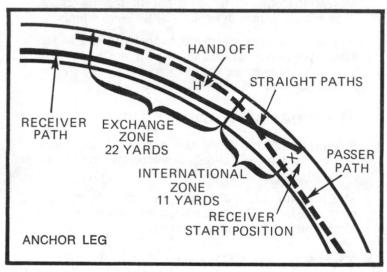

HAND OFF

H

STRAIGHT PATHS

RECEIVER PATH

EXCHANGE ZONE 22 YARDS

PASSER PATH

INTERNATIONAL ZONE 11 YARDS

RECEIVER START POSITION

ANCHOR LEG

The Anchor Sprinter

The **fourth runner** on the team should be your best competitive runner. She should have outstanding acceleration, a special ability to receive the baton and run under pressure, then finish with good technique.

The anchor runner begins her sprint from the International mark and receives the baton in her right hand as soon as possible after entering the exchange zone. The fourth sprinter runs the remaining distance of 114 yards to complete the 440-yard Sprint Relay race.

1. PRACTICE BATON EXCHANGE OFTEN.

Distance Baton Pass

In races over 4 x 200-yard legs, the outgoing runner must start and receive the baton within the 22-yard passing zone area.

The distance from the go mark to the point of exchange will vary according to the speed of the incoming runner.

The receiver should take off with three quick steps then look back and adjust her speed to the incoming runner. A go mark of about four yards back is standard.

The same style of hand-off should be used as in the sprint.

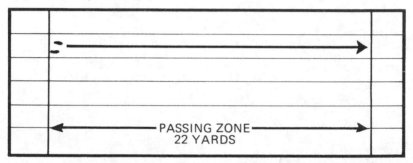

PASSING ZONE
22 YARDS

1. START AND RECEIVE BATON WITHIN 22-YARD EXCHANGE ZONE.
2. RECEIVER EXTENDS HAND BACK (LEFT) WITH WRIST "COCKED" FORWARD, LOOKS OVER HER SHOULDER AND ADJUSTS HER SPEED TO INCOMING RUNNER.
3. AT POINT OF EXCHANGE, OUTGOING RUNNER MAY CHOOSE TO LOOK; HOWEVER, MANY TEAMS PREFER TO USE THE "BLIND PASS" WHEREBY THE OUTGOING RUNNER KEEPS HER EYES FORWARD.

or

finish at the tape

Sprinters have numerous ways of breaking the tape at the finish of a race. Some use a shoulder lean while others duck their head against the tape. However, officials do not favor this type of finish because the rules governing the finish of a race state otherwise.

An athlete is declared a winner at the finish when she touches the tape with the chest area only. Breaking or striking the tape with the hand or the head does not declare that the runner has finished her race.

A runner should practice "bolting," "thrusting," "surging" or "exploding" into the tape and at the finish line so her timing will be at the correct, precise position of the finish line, not before or after.

As a sprinter approaching the end of your race, concentrate on position, timing and exploding into the tape. Your hands should be stretched back almost level to the track with palms down. The head is tilted back by pushing the chin up. This will force the chest forward. At this moment, the body in co-ordination with the legs will lean forward as the driving leg extends with power so you are thrust into the tape with an accelerated split-second "bolting action." ("Bolting" is the term used by navy airmen when planes are shot from catapults.)

Do not continue in this position more than one or two steps after crossing the finish line. Return to a normal running position to avoid a possible fall.

1. APPROACH TAPE IN FULL SPRINT POWER.
2. START BOLTING ACTION BY EXTENDING ARMS BACK AND PULL CHIN UP.
3. ARMS ARE EXTENDED FULLY BACK, PALMS DOWN. PULL CHIN UP, FORCE CHEST OUT AND INCREASE LEAN SO AS TO FORCE DRIVING LEG TO THE FINISH LINE.
4. AFTER BOLTING THROUGH TAPE, RETURN TO NORMAL RUNNING BY SYNCHRONIZING ARM ACTION WITH LEG ACTION. FAILURE TO DO SO WILL RESULT IN A RUNNER'S FALLING.
5. LET MOMENTUM CARRY INTO AN EASY SLOW-TO-STOP POSITION.

long jump

"Hitch Kick" Style

The Approach

The distance of the run to the takeoff board varies among athletes depending upon the ability to reach top speed and arrive at the board in a relaxed and controlled state. Usually, the approach distance is between 30 and 40 yards.

Markers should be placed at the start of the approach run and at a distance some 30 feet from the takeoff board. The marker at the beginning insures that the start is undertaken from the same spot each time. The second marker is used as a checkpoint for the run to the takeoff board.

Experiment to find the best approach distance for you. After you have fully determined this distance, the second marker probably will become less important.

1. **PLACE MARKERS AT START AND APPROXIMATELY 30 FEET FROM TAKEOFF BOARD.**
2. **USE MARKERS TO MAKE APPROACH RUN CONSISTENT.**
3. **RUN WITH SPEED AND CONTROL.**

Gather

Within the last three strides, prepare for the takeoff. On the next to the last step, lower your hips with a "dip" action to prepare for the spring lift. The last stride is shortened. Allow the body to come directly over the takeoff foot for maximum lift. To jump far, you first must jump upward.

Straighten your back and raise your chin. Do not look at the board at takeoff.

4. **THE STEP BEFORE TAKEOFF, LOWER HIPS WITH "DIP" ACTION AND DROP CENTER OF GRAVITY FOR "SPRING" UPWARD.**

5. **SHORTEN LAST STRIDE, TO ALLOW BODY TO COME DIRECTLY OVER TAKEOFF FOOT.**

6. **STRAIGHTEN BACK AND RAISE CHIN. DON'T LOOK AT BOARD AT TAKEOFF.**

Takeoff and Landing

Contact the board with a heel-ball-toe action. The knee is flexed then straightened to drive off the ball of the foot.

If driving off the left foot, the left arm and right knee drive upward and forward. For maximum height, rotate right arm.

Extend the left leg then repeat with the right. Rotate the left arm to coordinate with right leg motion. Extend in air as long as possible.

To land, extend arms and legs toward the end of the pit. Arms are extended above hip level. Land on your heels with legs together. Flex the knees upon contact and drop the chin downward to thrust weight forward and down.

Forward momentum should carry you over to your hands and knees.

7. **CONTACT BOARD WITH HEEL-BALL-TOE ACTION.**

8. WHEN DRIVING OFF LEFT FOOT, LEFT ARM AND RIGHT KNEE DRIVE UPWARD AND FORWARD. JUMP UP FIRST, NOT FORWARD.

9. EXTEND LEFT LEG THEN REPEAT WITH RIGHT. COORDINATE ARM AND LEG ACTION. EXTEND IN AIR AS LONG AS POSSIBLE.

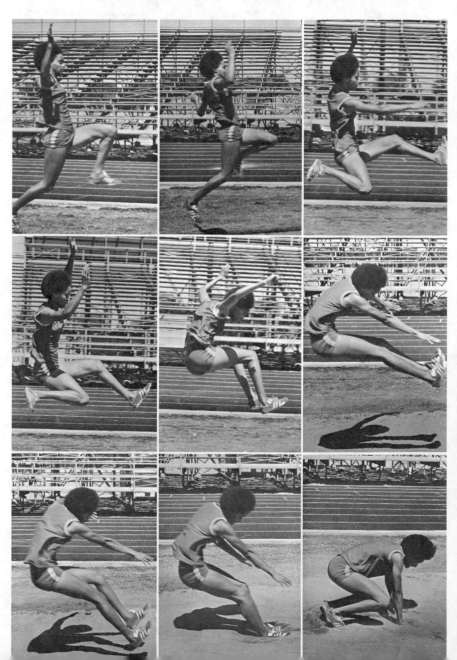

10. EXTEND ARMS AND LEGS TOWARD END OF PIT TO LAND.

11. LAND ON HEELS WITH LEGS TOGETHER. FLEX KNEES SLIGHTLY AND DROP CHIN DOWNWARD.

12. WEIGHT SHIFTS FORWARD TO CARRY YOU OVER HANDS AND KNEES.

"Hang" Style

The techniques of the "hang" style method of jumping are similar to those of the "Hitch Kick" style only that at maximum height the legs hang down or slightly back.

Drive off the takeoff foot as the opposite arm and leg thrust upward. At maximum height, the legs hang down and slightly back as the arms are held high overhead.

Swing the arms and feet forward into a sit-out position preparatory to landing.

1. DRIVE OFF TAKEOFF FOOT AS OPPOSITE ARM AND LEG THRUST UPWARD.

2. LEGS HANG DOWN AND SLIGHTLY BACK AT MAXIMUM HEIGHT OF JUMP.

3. SWING ARMS AND FEET FORWARD FOR LANDING.

high jump

Straddle Roll PROPERTY OF SCHOOL DISTRICT NO. 75

As a rule the high-jumping event allows athletes to develop some techniques which vary slightly from the standard.

However, the beginning high jumper first should attempt to adopt those fundamental techniques which have proven successful for most athletes then apply individual skills to refine and improve jumping ability.

Straddle Roll Techniques

Some coaches prefer to start the beginning jumper with the *Western Roll style* in preparation for *Straddle Roll* method. Using the Western Roll, the jumper clears the bar with legs somewhat together and with the side of the body facing the bar. Utilizing the Straddle Roll the jumper rotates around the bar with legs extended in a "spread-eagle" fashion and with the stomach facing toward the bar.

Most coaches begin the athlete with the Straddle Roll.

The Approach

The angle of approach to the crossbar is usually about 30 degrees but varies among athletes from 15 to 45 degrees, depending upon the style of the jump.

Most jumpers use a seven or nine step approach run. Speed often depends upon the individual's jumping style. Generally, you should have a strong half-speed stride until the final three steps when you then "drive harder" under control for the takeoff.

1. APPROACH BAR FROM APPROXIMATELY 30-DEGREE ANGLE TO CROSSBAR.

Gather for the Takeoff

Begin gather for the takeoff three strides from the takeoff point.

On the **second step** from the takeoff point, flex the outside knee and lower hips.

On **the third and last step,** begin strong arm action with elbows bent at 90 degrees and with palms out so as to force the action of the arms upward as the outside leg kicks with a hard, high, pendulum-type action.

The elbows come down as the hips sink to the lowest point.

2. BEGIN GATHER AT A DISTANCE OF THREE STRIDES FROM TAKEOFF POINT AND PREPARE ARMS FOR LIFT BY TURNING PALMS OUT AT SHOULDER HEIGHT.

3. ON SECOND STEP FROM TAKEOFF POINT, FLEX OUTSIDE KNEE. LOWER HIPS TO DROP CENTER OF GRAVITY. BRING ARM AND PALMS DOWN.

4. ON THIRD STEP, BEGIN STRONG ARM ACTION UPWARD WITH A "SCOOPING" ACTION HIGH ABOVE HEAD.

Takeoff

With the body leaning backward and the hips settled at the lowest point, plant the inside heel with the foot turned toward the bar about 18 inches away.

The last step is well ahead of the body. Drive the outside leg, hip and arm upward above but not toward the bar. Many jumpers become discouraged because they fail to learn this upward-thrust action properly.

The pendulum motion or kick action of the outside leg helps to lift the hips. At the highest point, straighten the outside leg.

One further note: right-handed jumpers usually prefer to jump off the left foot, whereas left-handed athletes most often choose to jump off the right foot.

5. LEAN BACK AND DROP HIPS TO LOWEST POINT. LAST STEP IS WELL AHEAD OF BODY.
6. PLANT INSIDE HEEL HARD WITH FOOT TURNED TOWARD CROSSBAR.
7. DRIVE OUTSIDE LEG, HIP AND ARM UPWARD, ABOVE BUT NOT TOWARD CROSSBAR.
8. STRAIGHTEN LEAD LEG AT HIGHER POINT.
9. TRAILING ARM SWINGS BACK SLIGHTLY TO HELP ROTATE BENT TRAILING LEG AROUND BAR.

Rotation and Landing

With outside leg, arm, head and shoulders above the level of the bar, rotate around the bar by driving the right shoulder over the head and extending the lead right arm downward.

The trailing arm swings back slightly to help rotate the bent trailing leg around the bar.

But some jumpers choose to tuck the trailing arm to the chest while straightening the trailing leg plus turning the toes out and away to pivot around the bar.

The rotation around the bar most likely will cause you to land on your back.

10. WITH OUTSIDE LEG, ARM, HEAD AND SHOULDERS ABOVE BAR, ROTATE AROUND BAR BY DRIVING RIGHT SHOULDER OVER HEAD AND EXTENDING RIGHT ARM DOWNWARD WITH PALM TURNED OUTWARD.
11. TRAILING ARM SWINGS BACK SLIGHTLY TO HELP ROTATE TRAILING LEG AROUND BAR.
12. LAND ON BACK TO COMPLETE JUMP.

"Fosbury Flop" Techniques

The *Fosbury Flop style* of jumping has gained acceptance and popularity within the past few years.

Dick Fosbury was the first to use this unique style of high jumping most successfully in the 1968 Olympic Games.

It is absolutely necessary to have a very large and soft pit since the jumper lands most often on the upper back and neck area. Injuries may very well occur if the pit is inadequate.

The Approach

Again, a seven or nine step approach is generally used. Most jumpers approach the bar three or four steps to the left of the perpendicular.

This style of jumping uses the speed generated during the approach run to good advantage. As always run with controlled speed.

1. USE SEVEN OR NINE STEP APPROACH TO BAR.
2. BEGIN APPROACH THREE OR FOUR STEPS TO THE RIGHT OR LEFT OF THE PERPENDICULAR AS YOU CHOOSE.
3. RUN FOR SPEED BUT WITH CONTROL.

Gather for Takeoff

The unique aspect of this jumping style is that the jumper clears the height with the back facing the bar rather than the stomach or side. Also, the jumper leaps off his outside leg rather than the inside leg.

Begin the gather at a distance of three strides from the bar. Do not turn your back to the bar too early but first drive the right knee and arms upward and jump off the left foot which is the outside foot.

While driving upward, turn the right shoulder slightly away from the bar thus starting the rotational movement of the back toward the bar. As the shoulder reaches a height over the bar, the rotation is such that the back faces the bar.

4. AT A DISTANCE OF THREE STRIDES FROM TAKEOFF POINT, BEGIN GATHER ACTION.

5. TWO STRIDES AWAY, LOWER HIPS TO DROP CENTER OF GRAVITY.

6. WITH THE FINAL STEP, PLANT OUTSIDE FOOT AND DRIVE INSIDE KNEE AND ARMS UPWARD.

7. WHILE DRIVING UP, TURN INSIDE SHOULDER SLIGHTLY AWAY FROM BAR. AS SHOULDER REACHES HEIGHT OVER BAR, ROTATE SO THAT BACK FACES BAR.

Above the Bar

Tip your head back to help arch the hips above the crossbar. As you clear the bar with the hips, raise your knees then straighten your forelegs to clear the bar.

Raising the knees and forelegs forces the hips downward. Therefore, it is necessary to wait until the hips are well clear of the bar before raising the knees and straightening the forelegs.

8. TIP HEAD BACK TO HELP ARCH THE BACK ABOVE THE CROSSBAR SO AS TO CLEAR HIPS OVER BAR.
9. WITH HIPS CLEAR OF BAR, RAISE KNEES AND THEN STRAIGHTEN FORELEGS TO CLEAR ALSO.

Landing

Land to cushion the fall on the upper portion of your back. Oftentimes after landing, the body continues on over in a somersault fashion.

Again, it is most important that the pit be large enough to avert possible injury.

10. LAND ON UPPER PORTION OF BACK. MOMENTUM MAY CARRY BODY OVER IN SOMERSAULT FASHION.

1. "FOSBURY FLOP" TECHNIQUE IS BECOMING
VERY POPULAR AMONG MANY JUMPERS
AND COACHES.

shot put

The Grip

Rest the shot at the base of the index and two middle fingers. The thumb and little finger provide support.

For optimum control place the little finger to the side of the shot. For greater power, move the little finger more behind the ball.

1. **REST SHOT AT BASE OF INDEX AND TWO MIDDLE FINGERS. DO NOT SPREAD FINGERS EXCESSIVELY.**
2. **THUMB AND LITTLE FINGER PROVIDE CONTROL AND SUPPORT.**

Starting Position

Place the shot in the hollow area adjacent to the rear process of the jaw. The elbow of the putting arm points forward and slightly downward to support the weight of the shot. The free arm should be relaxed with the hand about eye level and elbow up.

A right-handed putter places the right foot to the back of the circle, flat upon the surface with toes close to the rim. Usually with the toes, the opposite foot makes light contact with the surface, some 16 to 20 inches from the right foot.

Balance is a prime consideration at this state.

With head up, focus your eyes on some object 10 to 15 feet in a line opposite the direction of the throw.

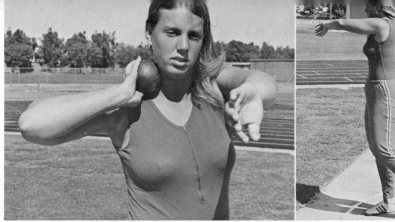

3. **HOLD SHOT AGAINST HOLLOW PROCESS ADJACENT TO JAW.**

4. **RIGHT FOOT IS FLAT UPON SURFACE WITH TOES CLOSE TO RIM. TOE OF LEFT FOOT CONTACTS SURFACE LIGHTLY, SOME 16 TO 20 INCHES BEHIND RIGHT FOOT.**

5. **HEAD UP WITH EYES FOCUSED ON POINT IN LINE DIRECTLY OPPOSITE TO DIRECTION OF THROW.**

Fly Action Across Ring

From the starting position, drop the center of gravity by flexing the right knee. Bring the left knee close to the planted leg as the head and upper body dip down. Make sure your weight is over the ball of the right foot.

Shift weight toward the center of the circle, by driving the left leg toward the toe board. Drive powerfully off the right leg; glide to the center of the circle. The right foot remains close to the surface of the ring but does not drag. Keep your head and eyes up.

Left and right feet should be planted almost simultaneously. Toes of the left foot touch the toe board while the heel forms a 10-degree angle with the board.

Continue the motion forward and do not dip the shot downward. Lead with the free arm and "pop" the hip in a forward, lifting motion. Turn the chin up and out as the shot starts forward.

6. **FROM STARTING POSITION, DROP CENTER OF GRAVITY BY FLEXING RIGHT KNEE.**

7. **BRING LEFT KNEE CLOSE TO PLANTED LEG AS HEAD AND UPPER BODY DIP DOWN.**

8. WEIGHT IS SUPPORTED ON BALL OF RIGHT FOOT.
9. WITH A QUICK MOTION, SHIFT WEIGHT BY DRIVING THE FREE LEG TOWARD THE TOE BOARD.
10. DRIVE OFF RIGHT FOOT TO GLIDE TO CENTER OF CIRCLE. DO NOT DRAG FOOT ON SURFACE. EXTEND LEFT LEG TOWARD TOE BOARD.

Release and Follow-Through

Shot remains against the neck as the elbow moves into a "high" position.

Keep the elbow high with foot in contact with the ground as long as possible.

Also, keep the shot moving in an upward, forward line to release the shot from the fingers with a distinct wrist snap. The motion of the chin is up and out as is the putting arm.

As the shot leaves the fingers, bring the rear foot forward to the toe board while shifting the left leg to the center of the circle. Lower hips to drop center of gravity over front foot, so as to stay in the ring after the "put."

Putting arm follows in a complete motion across the body. Keep the head in line with the throw.

10. KEEP ELBOW HIGH WITH BOTH FEET IN CONTACT WITH SURFACE AS LONG AS POSSIBLE. LEFT FOOT BRACED AS FULCRUM FOR DELIVERY ACTION. DRIVE UPWARD OFF BENT RIGHT LEG UTILIZING POWER OF TRUNK AND LEG MUSCLES.

11. KEEP SHOT MOVING IN AN UPWARD, FORWARD LINE. ACCELERATE WITH CONTINUOUS MOTION. RELEASE SHOT FROM FINGERS WITH DISTINCT SNAP OF WRIST.

12. DROP CENTER OF GRAVITY OVER FRONT LEG. PUTTING ARM FOLLOWS THROUGH TO COMPLETE MOTION ACROSS BODY. HEAD REMAINS IN LINE WITH THROW.

13. WORK TO ACHIEVE RHYTHM AND POWER NECESSARY TO THROW SHOT SUCCESSFULLY.

discus

The Grip

Slide the palm of the throwing hand across the face to grip the discus at the first joints of the four fingers. For greater finger strength and control, the first and second fingers should be held more closely together.

The thumb rides atop the discus with firm pressure for control.

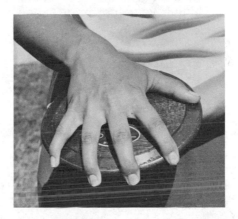

1. PALM OF THROWING HAND FLAT UPON FACE OF DISCUS.

2. FINGERS SPREAD, FIRST JOINT OF FINGERS "GRIPPING" EDGE WITH THUMB ON TOP PRESSING DOWN.

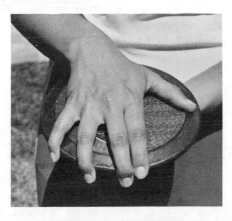

3. OR, INDEX AND 2ND FINGER TOGETHER WITH 3RD AND 4TH FINGER SPREAD.

Starting Position

Stand to the rear edge of the ring, facing the direction opposite to the intended throw. Spread your feet about 18 inches apart. Keep your weight over the right leg and take a few relaxed arm swings and body rotations without shifting your feet prior to the spin.

4. STAND TO REAR OF RING IN DIRECTION OPPOSITE TO INTENDED THROW WITH FEET SPACED ABOUT 18 INCHES APART.

5. WITHOUT MOVING FEET, TAKE SEVERAL ARM SWINGS AND BODY ROTATIONS.

Spin

Lead with the left knee into the circle. Pivot on the ball of the left foot while shifting your weight over the left foot. Throwing arm trails the entire turning movement. Look over the left shoulder toward the direction of the throw and drive the right foot to the center of the circle.

With a pronounced forward shoulder lean, bring the right leg around the left leg, leading with the knee. Keep the arm straight and the disc trailing the body action. Do not let the discus get too close to the body otherwise the discus will be too high in flight.

Both feet come off the ground momentarily, landing very quickly with the right then the left. The right foot lands approximately in the middle of the circle facing about the same direction as when starting.

Rear to Front View

6. LEAD WITH LEFT KNEE, PIVOT ON BALL OF LEFT FOOT AND SHIFT WEIGHT OVER LEFT FOOT. THROWING ARM TRAILS TURNING MOTION.

Front to Rear View

7. BRING RIGHT LEG AROUND LEFT, LEADING WITH THE KNEE. KEEP ARMS STRAIGHT AND DISCUS CLOSE TO HIPS.

8. BOTH FEET COME OFF GROUND MOMENTARILY, LANDING FIRST THE RIGHT THEN THE LEFT. RIGHT FOOT LANDS IN CENTER OF CIRCLE FACING STARTING DIRECTION.

Release and Follow-Through

The left foot serves as a braced fulcrum to complement the right-leg and hip-thrust action.

With weight over the right leg, drive off the right leg leading with the left hip and arm. Keep the shoulders, right arm and discus back as long as possible. Do not let the discus come forward during the spin, otherwise you lose power.

Pull discus from far behind the body with trunk and shoulders leading the movement. Keep the discus out and away from the body to make the release at shoulder height in front of the chest.

Snap shoulders and hips at the release while pressing the thumb downward.

As the discus leaves the throwing hand and fingers, rotate the rear foot forward and release the opposite foot to swing to the rear.

Lower hips dropping the center of gravity over the front foot to keep within the ring. The throwing arm follows in a complete motion across the body.

9. WITH WEIGHT OVER BRACED RIGHT LEG, DRIVE OFF RIGHT LEG LEADING WITH LEFT ARM AND HIP. KEEP DISCUS BACK AS LONG AS POSSIBLE.

10. PULL DISCUS FROM FAR IN BACK OF BODY WITH TRUNK AND SHOULDERS LEADING MOVEMENT.

11. **KEEP DISCUS OUT AND AWAY FROM BODY TO RELEASE AT SHOULDER HEIGHT IN FRONT OF CHEST.**

12. **SNAP SHOULDERS AND HIPS AT RELEASE WHILE PRESSING THUMB DOWN ON DISCUS AND KEEPING WRIST STRAIGHT.**

13. **UPON RELEASE, ROTATE REAR FOOT FORWARD AND RELEASE OPPOSITE FOOT TO SWING TO REAR. LOWER HIPS TO DROP CENTER OF GRAVITY OVER FRONT FOOT TO KEEP WITHIN RING.**

14. **PRACTICE OFTEN TO DEVELOP RHYTHM, POWER AND RELEASE NECESSARY TO SUCCESSFUL DISCUS THROWING.**

Side View

javelin

The Grip

Place the javelin diagonally in the palm of the hand. The palm grips the javelin with the index finger or index and second fingers wrapped around the shaft at the end of the cord.

Grip the javelin just tightly enough to maintain control.

1. **PLACE JAVELIN DIAGONALLY IN PALM OF HAND.**

2. **GRIP WITH PALM AND WRAP INDEX FINGER OR INDEX AND SECOND FINGER AROUND SHAFT AT CORD.**

3. **OR, THUMB AND INDEX FINGER ON SHAFT AT CORD.**

4. **OR, INDEX FINGER ALONG SHAFT OF JAVELIN WITH "STRONG" 2ND FINGER ON SHAFT AT THE CORD. (THIS METHOD SEEMS MORE POPULAR ALTHOUGH OTHER GRIPS ARE USED BY MANY TOP JAVELIN THROWERS.)**

Approach Run

Generally, a starting mark about 30 yards from the toe board is measured. Check points should be marked about the final 10 yards for the five final-throwing steps.

While increasing the speed of the run generates power, it should be kept in mind that excessive speed makes it difficult to stop. Speed must be generated but controlled to insure good body control during the final five steps.

5. DURING APPROACH, HOLD JAVELIN AT HEAD LEVEL OVER SHOULDER AND PARALLEL WITH GROUND.

Carry Position

When starting the approach, hold the javelin about ear level over the shoulder and parallel with the ground.

Upon reaching the final mark about 10 yards from the toe board, pull the javelin back, extending the arm fully. During the **first two steps of the final five-step approach** the javelin tip is at eye level with the tail up.

6. DRAW JAVELIN BACK, EXTENDING ARM FULLY UPON REACHING 10-YARD MARK FROM TOE BOARD.

Final Five-Step Approach

Like the first step of the final five-step approach, **the third stride** is a crossover step. For the right-handed thrower, this step is made by crossing the right leg over the left ahead of the body.

The fourth step is a long stride made with the left leg to plant the heel. This leg is used as a fulcrum over which the throwing action is made.

As the throw is made, the body extends forward and upward in the direction of the javelin's flight.

The right foot then comes forward for the follow-through which constitutes **the fifth step.** The right knee is flexed and the hips lowered to control the forward motion of the body and to prevent crossing the toe board.

7. JAVELIN TIP BROUGHT EVEN WITH EYE DURING FIRST TWO STEPS.

8. THIRD STEP IS CROSSOVER STEP USED TO HELP GET BODY INTO THROWING POSITION.

9. FOURTH STEP IS LONG STRIDE WITH LEFT LEG TO PLANT HEEL. LEFT LEG ACTS AS FULCRUM OVER WHICH THROW ACTION IS MADE.

10. AFTER THROW, RIGHT LEG COMES THROUGH FOR FIFTH AND FINAL STEP.

Throwing Action

Turn the chest toward the javelin to facilitate the full arm extension. With the final crossover step the leg is positioned in such a way that the toe points inward toward the runway. Weight is over the rear leg.

Lean back as far as possible while maintaining forward momentum. As the front foot strides forward the rear foot initiates throwing motion. Hips then rotate followed by the trunk, shoulders and finally the throwing arm. The arm pulls straight over the shoulder with the elbow leading the hand.

Release the javelin while rotating up and over the extended forward leg. Note that head and chin drop slightly away from the javelin; however, all action is upward and forward to the direction of flight.

11. **TURN CHEST TOWARD JAVELIN.**
12. **LEAN BACK ON REAR LEG, BUT MAINTAIN FORWARD MOMENTUM.**
13. **INITIATE THROWING MOTION WITH REAR FOOT. HIPS ROTATE FOLLOWED BY TRUNK, SHOULDERS AND THROWING ARM. ARM PULLS STRAIGHT OVER SHOULDER WITH ELBOW LEADING HAND AND CHEST FORWARD.**

14. RELEASE JAVELIN, ROTATING UP AND OVER EXTENDED FORWARD LEG.

15. COMPLETE THROW AND FOLLOW-THROUGH. CONTINUE REAR LEG FORWARD TO PLANT FOOT AT 90-DEGREE ANGLE TO DIRECTION OF THROW. FLEX KNEE OF REAR LEG AND DROP LEVEL OF HIPS TO SLOW MOMENTUM.

dimensions

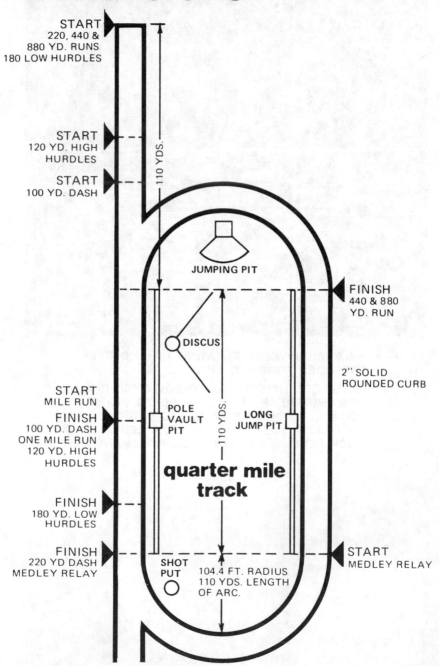

START
220, 440 &
880 YD. RUNS
180 LOW HURDLES

START
120 YD. HIGH
HURDLES

START
100 YD. DASH

110 YDS.

JUMPING PIT

FINISH
440 & 880
YD. RUN

DISCUS

2" SOLID
ROUNDED CURB

START
MILE RUN

FINISH
100 YD. DASH
ONE MILE RUN
120 YD. HIGH
HURDLES

POLE
VAULT
PIT

LONG
JUMP PIT

110 YDS.

quarter mile track

FINISH
180 YD. LOW
HURDLES

FINISH
220 YD DASH
MEDLEY RELAY

START
MEDLEY RELAY

SHOT
PUT

104.4 FT. RADIUS
110 YDS. LENGTH
OF ARC.

74

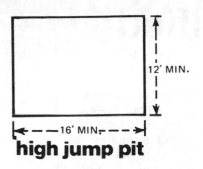

high jump pit

12' MIN.

16' MIN.

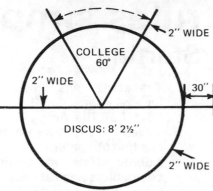

2" WIDE

COLLEGE
60°

2" WIDE

30"

DISCUS: 8' 2½"

2" WIDE

discus throw circle

2" WIDE

2" WIDE
2" WIDE

60°

30"

DIA. 7'

shot put circle

shot put toe board

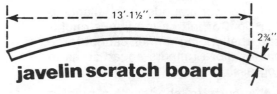

4½"

RADIUS 3'-6"

4"

4'

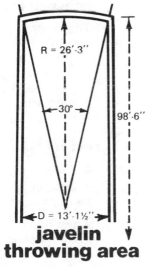

R = 26'-3"

30°

98'-6"

D = 13'-1½"

javelin throwing area

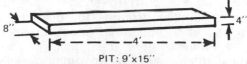

13'-1½"

2¾"

javelin scratch board

8"

4"

4'

PIT: 9'x15"

long jump take off board

Minimum 130' Runway Recommended

rules simplified
Starting

The starter shall give the following commands for every race: 1) "Runners Go to Your Marks" 2) "Set," 3) The Firing of the Gun. If a competitor leaves her mark with hand or foot after the "set" position but before the shot is fired, it shall be considered a false start. On the command "set" all competitors shall at once and without delay assume their full and final "set" position. Failure to comply with this command after a reasonable time shall constitute a false start, and the runner shall be warned by the starter that if she makes another false start she will be disqualified from the race.

The runner must place her hands behind the starting line; prior to the shooting of the starting pistol the runner may not touch this line or any of the area in front of it. The runners may use starting blocks for their feet but both feet must be in contact with the track when starting.

Running

A runner shall be disqualified from a race who jostles, cuts across or otherwise obstructs a competitor so as to impede her progress.

When running around one or more curves, a runner cannot gain advantage by stepping on or over her lane line three or more consecutive steps.

A leading runner cannot impede a challenging competitor to her right or left on the final straightaway. Likewise, a challenging runner cannot force her way past one or more runners ahead so as to impede their progress.

Stepping onto the curb to shorten the running distance constitutes grounds for disqualification as does having a teammate, coach or spectator assist the runner before the finish of the race. Assisting a runner shall mean running alongside to shout encouragement or physically helping a runner.

Once a runner leaves the track voluntarily before the finish of a race, she cannot return to that race.

Hurdles

A hurdler may knock down any number of hurdles without being disqualified from the race. However, a competitor who runs around or carries her leg or foot alongside any hurdle shall be disqualified.

For the rules which govern the starting of a hurdle race refer to the foregoing rules-simplified section entitled "Starting."

Relay Race

The same rules and penalties apply to relay race competition as for other running events.

If any member of a relay team is disqualified, the team is disqualified.

A runner may carry the baton in either hand, but cannot transport it otherwise. The baton must be passed within the 22-yard passing zone.

After passing the baton, a runner cannot veer into another lane so as to impede the progress of a competitor.

The Long Jump

In a meet involving two teams, each individual is allowed four jumps. The best of the four jumps is the competitor's record for that meet. In a meet involving more than two teams each competitor is allowed three jumps in the finals. The number of qualifiers for the finals corresponds to the number of awards to be given plus one. Example: If five medals are to be awarded then six competitors will qualify for the finals. If a jumper has a better jump in the preliminaries than in the finals, the preliminary jump shall count as her best for the meet.

If any part of the foot touches the ground on the pit side of the takeoff board during the takeoff, the jump is considered a foul, and as such will not be measured but will count as an attempt. Also, if the jumper runs past the takeoff board, a foul is recorded.

The measurement of the jumps shall be made at right angles from the takeoff board to the nearest break in the ground (pit) made by the individual.

The High Jump

The high jumper is allowed three attempts at each height. If she misses one height with three consecutive jumps, she is eliminated from the competition, whereas the best height which she successfully cleared is listed as her record for that day. If the jumper runs at the bar, decides not to jump but runs under the bar, an attempt is registered. If any part of her body projects under or over the bar, an attempt is counted.

A jumper must jump off one foot.

The Shot Put

The shot putter is allowed to throw the shot from within a circle with a diameter of seven feet. At no time during the throw may she step either on the boundary of the circle or step out of the circle. After she has made her throw, she must walk out of the back half of the circle. In a meet which only involves two teams, each competitor is allowed four throws. In a meet with many teams entered, each competitor is allowed three throws in the preliminaries, and if qualifying for the finals, three throws in the finals. The number of qualifiers is determined by adding one place to the number of places which will count as scores.

The Discus

The discus thrower must throw from within a circle having a diameter eight feet 2½ inches. In making her throw, the thrower must not touch the edge of the circle or the ground outside of it with any part of her body. She must not leave the circle until the discus has landed and she must leave from a standing position from the rear half of the circle.

The measurement must be made from the nearest edge of the mark first made in the ground by the discus to the inner edge of the circle along a line drawn from the mark to the center of the circle. The discus must land within a sector which forms a 60-degree angle extended from the center of the circle.

The Javelin

The javelin shall consist of three parts: a metal head, a shaft and a cord grip. The shaft may be constructed of either wood or metal.

The javelin must be held by the grip, with one hand only, and so that the little finger is nearest to the point. The thrower's last contact with the javelin shall be with the grip.

At no time after preparing to throw until the javelin has been thrown in the air may the competitor turn completely around so that her back is toward the throwing area. The javelin shall be thrown ovor the shoulder or upper part of the throwing arm and may not be thrown with an underhand motion.

No throw shall be valid or counted in which the tip of the point of the javelin does not strike the ground before any other part of the shaft.

For complete rules contact:
Division for Girls' and Women's Sports
1201 Sixteenth St., N.W.
Washington, D.C. 20036

Training for the Distance Run

The following is a suggested training format for a period leading up to and immediately following a competitive event. It should be noted that the sections of the workouts correspond to the sections of a particular running event.

1st Day: (Base Work)

A distance runner can begin her basic preparations by running with a moderately paced stride. This running insures that proper stress is placed on development of her running muscles and breathing technique. This is accomplished by interval work of any distance which adds up to about four times the intended racing distance. For example, 880-yard runners would run sixteen 220-yard runs at a pace near racing speed. However, this is subject to the opinion of the coach. In addition, a "second effort" segment should be added to the workout consisting of a 20- to 30-minute long-distance run with pickups of 165- to 220-yard hard strides. There should be at least two pickups for each five minutes out.

2nd Day: (Running Form)

The distance runner should run in terrain which has both slight and steep inclines of at least 30 to 60 yards in length to force correct, violent-arm action, power-leg action, head and body position. This training method will insure the correct type of running action for the final drive to the finish line during the last one-eighth or one-quarter of a race.

The athlete should run in terrain which has a slight decline of at least 120 to 160 yards at seven-eighths speed to develop increased hip relaxation and improvement in stride distance.

If hills are not available, the runner can accomplish almost the same thing by working against heavy winds for arm and leg power and by running with the wind to develop relaxed hip action and increased leg stride action.

3rd Day: (Over-Distance Training)

To attain endurance for a certain distance, the runner should run her distance under a controlled pace (a little slower than regular pacing) then push herself with at least one quarter more distance at a sprint pace. This accomplishes one of the basic conditioning methods, that of "tire the muscle, then make it work." An athlete can make two or three of these controlled runs with added sprint distance during a training session. Example: 880 + 220 = 1100 yards.

Many times the runner will respond to a degressive type of over-distance workout.

Example: 880 + 220
660 + 220
440 + 220
220 + 220

A runner should play a game of adding the four 220 yards together to break the two-minute time in the 220-yard run.

4th Day: (Race Tune-Up)

Two days before a track meet, the runner concentrates on under-distance speed work. Most of the speed drills should be built around sharpening the individual for her particular race. A great deal of time is spent on running particular phases of each race.

In the case of the 440, for example, the runner could spend the first phase of her workout perfecting her technique for coming out of the starting blocks and for going into the first turn. During the second phase of her workout, time may be spent working on the skills involved in running on a turn, hugging the inside line, entering a curve and coming out of a curve. The third phase of the workout might consist of running the straightaways with a hard stride and walking the curves. The fourth and final phase of the workout should be concerned with the last 88 yards of the 440, which is an all-out sprint. The four phases of the workout correspond to the four phases of the 440, and in this way the runner can cover all the skills involved in the race through the workout on her tune-up day.

Girls who run the 880 and the mile should also work on some additional skills, such as passing other runners. Also, a great deal of time should be spent working on certain areas of her race. For example, 880 girls would run a paced 550, rest, and then run at a faster pace between 550 and 792 yards. The girls should try to drop the time on this phase of the race by at least a second or two. The last phase of the tune-up is concentrated on running the last 88 yards in an all-out sprint and breaking the tape. In checking over the tune-up day workouts, again it should be noted that these workouts correspond to each phase of a race.

5th Day: Rest Day

Generally the day before a track meet, the athletes should be allowed to decide exactly what type of workout they would like to do. In many cases the athlete would rather take a complete rest during this time, whereas other athletes find it necessary to take a light run on grass. These runs could be at a number of distances. The coach must be very careful in analyzing his runners. Some runners may need as much as 48 to 60 hours rest before competition, where others perform better with around 36 to 48 hours rest. All individuals are different and must be treated individually. There is no set workout for a rest day since all individuals prepare themselves physically, mentally and psychologically in different ways during this time.

6th Day: (Day of Competition)

The individual should try to keep herself in as much of a relaxed atmosphere as possible. Each person has her own way of finding relaxation during a possible tension period. Most runners seem to do better when they refrain from being involved in conversations with athletes other than their own group. Radios have a tendency to take the athletes' minds off the coming race and relieve some of the tension. Reading helps some while just lying down and resting in a quiet place seems to soothe others. If the athlete has two or more races to run, it would be a good idea for her to enjoy complete rest in between by lying down with her feet elevated above the heart in a completely relaxed position.

If the day is exceptionally hot and humid, it is very important that the athlete sip water or tea so that her blood volume will remain normal. A hungry but moist athlete performs better than a full, dry one.

7th Day: (Following Competition)

Athletes should find an interesting, cool, soft area to run distance-style for a period of one to 1½ hours. A variety of different running areas from week to week tends to revive the enthusiasm of the runner. This time should be spent with two or more running partners but not under the coach's supervision.

Conditioning

Girls should start double workouts 37 days prior to national competition. One of the daily sessions should be devoted to *Fartlek workouts** of one or 1½ hours. They should return to single daily workouts prior to competition. The athletes may ease up in intensity of a normal week's work just prior to a national meet.

The coach and the individual must have a thorough understanding of the races to be run.

*See glossary of track and field terms.

Special Note about Workouts

A workout program must be built on a yearly basis. It should be complemented by a strong cross-country program for runners and a good running program for field event competitors. Interest should be kept alive during the indoor season.

Women track athletes should plan to start the early spring season with approximately the same marks as they finished around the time of the previous outdoor nationals. A period of easing off during July and August is recommended. During this period, workouts should be decreased to about one every other day.

Competitive Meets

A successful track program must strive to bring together the best athletes in all state, national and international meets depending upon their ability. Failure to raise the necessary funds or to show an interest in getting the athletes into high class meets throughout the United States will have a definite deteriorating effect on a club program. If a program is worth running, it is worth running 100 per cent. Many of the programs and coaches in the United States are active on a seasonal basis. A successful program cannot survive under these conditions.

Special Notes about Body Function

SALT CONTENT—It is very important that a coach check his or her athletes for the correct **salt intake** during hot and humid days. He should constantly encourage them to include the necessary minerals during their diet program.

IRON CONTENT—The **iron content** in the body must be kept at a normal level at all times, otherwise the athlete will be running below normal level efficiency because of a low blood count. It takes some systems as much as three weeks to become accustomed to surplus iron intake, then it must be maintained regularly as prescribed in the following diet.

FAT CONTENT—**The fat** contained in the blood stream must be kept to an absolute minimum so that maximum oxygen and nutrition may be carried.

LIQUID—Normal **intake of liquids** should be maintained at all times and special care should be made during competitive days. Many athletes fail to keep their blood volume at a normal level during competition and, because of this, they fail to perform normally.

Diet Considerations for Women Track Athletes

A training diet to a good track girl is the determining factor as to whether she runs up to her maximum capacity or below.

Iron, calcium, and phosphorous are basic food elements necessary to a balanced athletic diet. **Iron** is very important, for lack of iron causes shortness of wind and excessive beating of the heart during exercise. Foods such as roast beef, beef kidney, liver, oysters, spinach, spinach juice, whole wheat bread, eggs and fresh fruit go far in supplying this demand. **Calcium** is a basic mineral needed for endurance. It neutralizes the waste products of muscular exercise and is a definite necessity for good distance performances. Eggs, peas, raisins, grapes, rice and milk are some of the foods which can give athletes their necessary calcium requirements. **Phosphorous** resists the onset of fatigue and is used in the process of efficient muscle contraction. Phosphorous is found in whole wheat, oatmeal, lima beans and raisins.

Along with these basic food elements, there are certain special diet considerations which will pay dividends in performance.

Fried or greasy foods and gooey pastries are definitely out. It takes 11% more digestive energy to digest fats than carbohydrates. Fats increase the acidity of the blood, therefore lower endurance.

Athletes should eat only at meal time and should not leave the table "stuffed." Candy without peanuts (such as hard rock candy) may be eaten immediately after the evening meal. In moderation cake and pie can be worked into a diet. Women track athletes must stay away from such food in the latter part of the week before competition. If one must eat between meals or before going to bed, fruit such as grapes, oranges, apples is suggested. However, apples are taboo before a workout or a meet, for they cause intense gas pains in the stomach and intestines. Honey, grapes, dates, and raisins contain sugar (fructose) for energy and possess laxative qualities. These foods should be in an athlete's diet at every meal if possible.

One quart of milk, partially skimmed, each day at breakfast is a minimum requirement. Eggs, boiled or poached, should be eaten three times a week at breakfast only. Two or three oranges a day are essential since they contain citric acid to ward off colds. Meat should be used sparingly.

Track athletes should strive to regulate the function of the body, and proper elimination of wastes is of greatest importance. The best time to perform this task is after breakfast. Food should be of sufficient bulk to fill the tract and food bulk should be spongy enough to move freely and easily.

Energy Foods for Activities

Carbohydrates are starches and sugars which are the easiest of all foods to digest. Both are "fuel to burn" when **speed is desired.** They are rapidly absorbed and produce energy. The best sources of carbohydrates are fruits, vegetables, cereals, bread, honey and plain hard candies. **Fats,** although high in food value, are digested and absorbed more slowly. Fats are the type of food to be avoided where speed is desired. Chief fat sources are rich milk, cream, butter, ice cream, fatty meats, gravies, bacon, nuts, eggs and vegetable oils.

Some extra **salt** is wise to take where sweating is a problem. Bouillon cubes are a good source of salt. If salt tablets are to be used, they should be taken with the pre-game meal and not just before the contest as the salt can irritate the stomach and cause vomiting.

One group of investigators seems to feel that extra dosages of **Vitamin B1 and B2** increase the length and speed of nerve reaction time.

Wind

Wind is a factor in a training diet. The diet must contain soda-like compounds which are found most abundantly in all fruits and vegetables and are concerned with the elimination of carbonic acid (exhaust gases) from the body. Lemonade, orange juice or any type of fruit juice well sweetened with malt, sugar or honey makes a fine drink to aid the elimination of the toxic carbonic acid from the lungs and preserve the athlete's wind.

In terms of the utilization efficiency of oxygen, it should be noted that one liter of oxygen yields five calories if used to burn carbohydrates, but only 4.5 calories if used to burn protein or fat. This is a 10 per cent difference in the utilization of oxygen and may be an important factor in competitive performance. So it would be a good idea to **avoid proteins** in great amounts before an event.

When to Eat

When to eat is an important factor in good athletic performances.

In general, the amount of time in which various foods leave the stomach is as follows:

Meat leaves the stomach 2½ to three hours after being eaten. Meat is best for a pre-contest meal and it doesn't make any difference whether it is cooked rare, medium or well-done; it remains in the stomach for the same amount of time. Pork takes much longer, liver hangs on for about 6 hours, ham stays on for 8 hours. Sweetbreads and weiners outstay ham. Eggs leave faster.

Vegetables such as peas, carrots, corn and beans take from two to 2½ hours to leave the body. Parsnips, cabbage, turnips, and onions take longer. Potatoes, whether they are boiled, baked, whipped or mashed, take the same time. **Pudding, light cakes, ice cream,** and **pies** empty in 2½ to three hours. Strange as it may seem, custard remains longer. Soft, new **bread** and **rolls** stay in the stomach a long time while **whole wheat toast** remains only a short time. **Coffee** and **tea** have no effect on emptying time. Tea (long duration) is a diuretic which increases the blood pressure and augments muscular energy while diminishing fatigue sense. Coffee (short duration) is stronger than tea. If an athlete likes coffee and tea and is used to them, use in moderation is acceptable. **Fruit juices** are always good, especially from citrus fruits. **Milk** should be consumed slowly and boiled milk is easier to digest. Milk should never be drunk on the day before a meet or the day of a meet. **Ice water always slows up and disturbs digestion.** It is advocated that water loss and intake should be pretty well balanced. In general, an athlete's water supply should be completed when she is fairly dry. That is, she should cut down somewhat on her liquids. Blood volume must be maintained. To do this, the track girl should sip liquids from time to time, **but not overdo it.**

Most experts agree that the worst thing an athlete can do is to go without breakfast. A light evening meal and a heavy breakfast are better for anyone who exercises as much as an athlete does. Athletes should reverse the usual order and have steaks for breakfast and cereals for supper.

It is extremely important for women track athletes to keep a maximum amount of iron in their bloodstreams. This can be accomplished through the use of **ferrous gluconate drugs** which can be purchased at any pharmacy. These women should take three pills daily starting three days before their menstrual periods and continue for 14 days.

It will take the athletes 30 days before the pills will start helping their systems. It is imperative that they do not miss a single day, since the blood count of women athletes should stay at the highest level at all times.

Daily Musts for Track Women

1. **Ferrous gluconate pills** to keep the iron level in the bloodstream.

2. A generous helping of **liver** at least twice a week.

3. **Raisins** or some **hard candies** to satisfy the urge for candy.

4. An ample supply of **wheatgerm** either in liquid or dry form.

5. Plenty of **sleep.**

6. Continuous use of **liquids and juices** to keep blood volume at its correct level.

7. Great intake of **salt and other minerals** to keep the body well supplied.

8. At least 500 M. G. of **Vitamin C** each day (pill.)

glossary of track and field terms

A.A.U.: Amateur Athletic Union.

ANCHOR: The final or fourth leg of a relay.

ANGLE OF DELIVERY: Angle to the ground at which an implement is released.

APPROACH: The run and/or adjustments made by the participant prior to the actual competitive effort.

BALL-HEEL-BALL: Method in which distance runners touch the foot to ground while running.

BARRIER: A term used for a hurdle.

BATON: A tubelike object of wood or metal which is passed from one runner to another in a relay race.

BLIND PASS: A relay pass with the outgoing runner receiving the baton without turning her head to look at the approaching runner.

BREAK: Leaving the starting blocks before the gun sounds.

CALISTHENICS: Simple exercises done to warm up and prepare the body for activity.

CHUTE: The prolongation of the straightaway of an oval or semioval track.

CIRCLE: Competitive area for the shot and discus.

CLOSED POSITION: A powerful throwing position for shot and discus throwers in which the right shoulder and hip are back.

CROSSBAR: The bar, which can be raised or lowered, placed between two standards for the high jump.

CUT-DOWN: The dropping of the lead leg when clearing the hurdle.

D.G.W.S.: Division for Girls' and Women's Sports—a counseling and governing body for women's sports.

DRIVE-LEG: The leg exerting the force during stride or takeoff.

FALSE START: Leaving the starting line before the starting signal is given.

FIELD: Area of participation, as contrasted with the running track.

FOLLOW-THROUGH: The movement of a part or parts of the body following movement.

FOUL: A competitive effort wasted due to an infraction of a rule.

FRONT CROSS: Finnish method of getting the body into position for javelin throwing.

FRONT RUNNER: One who can run well leading and setting pace.

GRIP: Hand hold on an implement for a competitive event.

HAND OFF: The passing of the baton from the incoming runner to the outgoing runner in a relay.

HEAD WIND: Wind blowing toward the athlete.

HIGH-JUMP STANDARDS: Uprights which are used to hold the crossbar for the high jump.

INTERCOLLEGIATE COMPETITION: Competition between institutions at the college level.

INTERSCHOLASTIC COMPETITION: Competition between institutions on the secondary school level.

JOGGING: Running at a slow pace.

KICK: Leg speed used at end of a race.

KICKER: Runner who depends upon kick to win.

LEAD LEG: The first leg to leave the ground in jumping. The first leg over the hurdle.

LEAD OFF: The first runner on a relay team.

LEG: A section of a relay. The distance run by a member of a team.

MARKS: An athlete's starting point for a race.

MEDLEY: A relay race in which the various "legs" are of unequal distance.

N.C.A.A.: National Collegiate Athletic Association.

N.F.S.H.S.A.A.: National Federation of State High School Athletic Associations.

PACE: The rate of covering ground while running.

PASSER: The relay runner who "hands off" the baton.

PASSING: Not taking one's jump or vault as it comes up.

PASSING ZONE: A zone in which a pass must be made during a relay.

PIT: An area filled with sawdust, sand or synthetic material into which a long jumper or high jumper lands.

PULL UP: Raising by pulling of the body in pole vaulting.

PURSUIT RELAY: A relay in which all runners run in the same direction.

RECEIVER: The person receiving the baton in a relay race.

RECOVERY LEG: The nondriving leg when running.

REFLEX: Automatic and involuntary muscle reaction.

REVERSE: The follow-through after a put or throw.

RHYTHM: Uniform, well coordinated running action.

SAILING: The body in suspension when crossing the hurdle.

SCISSORS JUMP: A method of high jumping in which the legs are moved as if opening and closing a scissors when crossing the bar.

SCRATCH LINE: The takeoff line which cannot be crossed in the throwing and some jumping events.

SHOT: Iron or brass spheres, 8, 12 or 16 pounds in weight, used for competition.

SHUTTLE RELAY: A relay where the legs are run back and forth over the same course. Half of each relay team is at opposite ends of the prescribed distance.

SPRING: Bounce or lightness of foot.

STANCE: Particular starting position of an athlete.

STANDARDS: Upright objects used to hold crossbars during jumping or vaulting contests.

STARTING BLOCKS: Equipment used by runners to obtain a reliable and firm support for a fast start.

STRADDLE ROLL: A method of high jumping by clearing the bar face down.

STRAIGHTAWAY: Straight area of the track from one curve to the next.

STRIDE: The distance covered by a leg cycle while running.

SWING: Pendulum action of the body or a part of the body.

TAKEOFF: Act of leaving ground as in hurdles, jump or vault.

TAKEOFF FOOT: Foot which drives athlete from the ground.

TAKEOFF MARK: Spot at which athlete leaves the ground.

TECHNIQUE: Form used to execute an action.

TOE BOARD: A restraining board for certain field events, such as the shot put and discus throw.

TOUCH OFF OR TAG: Touching a relay runner rather than passing a baton, as in shuttle races.

WARM UP: Gradual process of raising the body temperature and loosening up muscles prior to strenuous exercise or competition.

WESTERN ROLL: Method of high jumping. Clearing the bar on the side or back.

WIND SPRINT: Practice sprint for conditioning purposes.

PROPERTY OF SCHOOL
DISTRICT NO. 75